MW00611023

DAD,
TELL ME

FROM:

_____

DATE:

_____

FOR YOU, BECAUSE:

_____

DAD,
TELL ME

A Give and Get Back Book

ELMA VAN VLIET

PARTICULAR BOOKS
an imprint of
PENGUIN BOOKS

For all children who receive the completed book:

Enjoy reading your father's stories.
I hope this becomes a true voyage of discovery.
About him, then and now, and about everything.

A NOTE FOR DAD

This is your book and your story. Feel free to make it completely your own!

You can decide how much and how often you write.

Rewrite questions if you'd like to answer them differently.

Add pictures you'd like to share.

Whatever feels right to you.

When you're done, give the book back to your daughter or son.

You've just shared the stories of a lifetime with someone who loves you.

CHILDHOOD

GROWING UP

ALL YOUR FAVOURITES

WHO YOU ARE NOW

CHILDHOOD

ABOUT BEING A CHILD

What day were you born? Were you born at home or in a hospital?

I was born on a Friday about 7 PM in a hospital. I believe it was St. Joseph's in St. Charles.

What is your full name? William Carl Wehmeier

Carl was my step-grandfather's name. Also the name of one of my god-parents — Carl Stille. My other god-father was Roland Wehmeier.

Do you know why your parents picked your name?

My mother's mother died three days after my mother was born and she was raised by the Stille family since my real maternal grand-father, Herbert Grossenheider, could not care for her.

My paternal grand-father was William Henry Casper Wehmeier.

What were your nicknames?

My nickname as a child was Billy which some of the older family members still called me. I much preferred Bill

Carl Stille was married to Herbert Grossenheider's sister.

Growing up on a farm which was somewhat isolated, I used to enjoy exploring the fields and looking for wildlife. Once my father (Elmer) caught a small fox which we tried to raise but it died shortly after being caught.

Both my sister (Jean) and I had assigned daily chores. Mine was to fill the drinking water bucket from the pump. I had the better chore since her's was to empty the nightly "chamber pot" since we did not have a bathroom, only an outhouse.

What imaginary games did you play as a child?

Cowboys and Indians. Also I would build "forts" out of hay bales in the hayloft of the barn.

Did you ever pretend to be a superhero? Which one?

ABOUT BEING A CHILD

How do you remember your childhood? *I was happy with a loving, Christian family.*

Did you, for example, have a favourite toy that you brought everywhere?

What people or things were important to you? *My parents and sisters. Also my grandfather Wehmeier who I was named after (William).*

I remember having chicken pox and being very sick with it.

NO

softball

What were your favourite games? + hobbies.

Did you play inside the house, or did you like to go outside?

A lot of my free time was spent building model airplanes from kits. Most were plastic and a few were wood. I especially liked WWII fighter planes.

Also, I enjoyed playing Monopoly with my friend John Willard every Saturday morning.

ABOUT BEING A CHILD

Who was your favourite playmate? _John Wilbrand_

What was your favourite day of the week?

Why was
this day
so special
to you?

Christmas — still is.

All my aunts & uncles from my mothers side (and cousins) would come to our house to exchange presents on Christmas Eve.

An old neighbor from down the road (Ernst Westerfeld) would be dressed as Santa and show up to give us kids our presents.

a page for
pictures . . .

. . . and more stories
and memories

a page for
pictures . . .

. . . and more stories
and memories

ABOUT YOUR
(GRAND)PARENTS

What are your parents' names? _____

_____

_____

_____

_____

Where and when were they born? _____

_____

_____

_____

Where and when were your grandparents born? _____

Grandmother and grandfather on your mother's side: _____

_____

_____

_____

_____

Grandmother and grandfather on your father's side: _____

_____

_____

_____

_____

Did you know your grandparents? Did you visit them often?

How was your extended family important to you while growing up?

ABOUT YOUR
(GRAND)PARENTS

What were different family members known for? _____

_____

Was anyone
in your family
famous?

_____

_____

_____

_____

_____

_____

_____

_____

Who was the black sheep? _____

_____

_____

_____

_____

_____

_____

_____

_____

What did your parents do for a living?

And your grandparents?

ABOUT YOUR
(GRAND)PARENTS

What kind of parents were your parents?

Were they
modern
or more
old-fashioned?

How would you describe their relationship?

Was it a
traditional
one?

What role did religion play in your parents' lives?

ABOUT YOUR
(GRAND)PARENTS

How did your parents spend their free time? _____

_____

_____

_____

_____

_____

_____

_____

_____

_____

_____

_____

_____

_____

_____

Do you look more like your mother or your father? _____

What features and traits did you inherit from each? _____

_____

How can
you tell? _____

_____

_____

What are the most important life lessons your parents taught you?

What activities did you enjoy doing with your father? What did you talk about?

And with your mother?

ABOUT YOUR
(GRAND)PARENTS

What kind of father was your father?

_____

_____

_____

_____

_____

_____

_____

_____

_____

Can you share some cherished memories about your father?

_____

_____

_____

_____

_____

_____

_____

_____

_____

_____

_____

What kind of mother was your mother?

Can you share some cherished memories about your mother?

a page for
pictures . . .

. . . and more stories
and memories

a page for
pictures . . .

. . . and more stories
and memories

ABOUT YOUR FAMILY

How many children did your parents have? _____

What are your brothers' and sisters' names? When were they born? _____

_____

_____

_____

_____

_____

_____

Growing up, who did you spend the most time with? _____

_____

How close
were you
to your
siblings?

_____

_____

_____

_____

_____

_____

_____

_____

Did you have any family pets? If so, what type? What were their names? _____

_____

_____

_____

What kind of family were you?

Did you like spending time at home?

How did you help around the house?

ABOUT YOUR FAMILY

Were there activities you always did together? What were they? _____

_____

_____

_____

_____

_____

_____

_____

What television programmes or films did you watch together? What books did you read? _____

_____

_____

What
programmes
did you enjoy
most?
_____

_____

_____

_____

What games did you like to play together? _____

_____

_____

_____

_____

What kind of house did you live in? What was the address?

Did you
ever move?

What did your room look like? Was it your own or did you share it?

What have you held on to from your childhood home?

ABOUT YOUR FAMILY

What kind of neighbourhood did you grow up in? _____

_____

_____

_____

Did you
know your
neighbours? _____

_____

_____

_____

_____

_____

How did you celebrate your birthday? _____

_____

_____

_____

_____

_____

_____

What was the best birthday present you ever received? _____

_____

_____

_____

What was your favourite food? And what did you hate?

What kind of food did your parents make? Do you cook like them now?

Are there any dishes you still make the same way your parents used to make them?

31

ABOUT YOUR FAMILY

Did you ever go on family holidays or take any trips? Where did you go?

Which of
these outings
still brings
a smile to
your face?

What were your favourite stay-at-home moments?

How did you celebrate Christmas?

What other special days did your family observe?

ABOUT YOUR FAMILY

As a family, how did you communicate your feelings?

_____

_____

_____

_____

Did you
talk a lot
or very
little?

_____

_____

_____

_____

_____

What hard times did you go through as a family?

_____

_____

_____

_____

_____

_____

_____

_____

_____

_____

Can you share some fond family memories?

a page for
pictures . . .

... and more stories
and memories

a page for
pictures . . .

. . . and more stories
and memories

ABOUT GROWING UP AND BECOMING AN ADULT

What primary school did you go to?

What secondary school did you go to?

Who was your favourite teacher?

Why was she or he special to you?

Did you have a teacher you hated? Why?

Were you a model student or did you dislike school?

What did you want to be when you were grown up?

Who were your best friends in primary school?

Do you still keep in touch with them?

ABOUT GROWING UP AND BECOMING AN ADULT

What was your favourite thing to do after school?

Did you have a lot of homework? Did you always do it?

Tell me one of your funniest memories of school.

What were your favourite subjects in school? Your least favourite?

Did you want to pursue higher education? Did your parents want the same for you?

ABOUT GROWING UP AND BECOMING AN ADULT

What did you think of secondary school? _____

_____

_____

_____

_____

_____

_____

_____

_____

_____

Did learning come easily to you, or was it hard? _____

_____

_____

_____

_____

_____

_____

_____

_____

_____

If you had the chance to organize a reunion, who would definitely get an invitation?

What were the most important world events as you were growing up?

ABOUT GROWING UP AND BECOMING AN ADULT

What were you like as a teenager? How did you see the world?

What did you look like? What styles were cool back then?

Did you try to fit in with a particular group or clique?

What were your dreams back then?

Did you
set any
goals for
yourself?

ABOUT GROWING UP AND
BECOMING AN ADULT

Who did you look up to growing up? Who were your idols?

What were your hobbies? Sports, music, collections?

What was your favourite band or artist?

Did you get pocket money, or did you have a job to earn some extra money?

How much spending money did you have each week?

What was your first real job?

How old were you when you started working? Do you remember how much you made?

What did you spend your first paycheque on?

49

ABOUT GROWING UP AND BECOMING AN ADULT

What later jobs did you hold?

_____

_____

_____

_____

_____

_____

_____

_____

_____

_____

Which of your jobs did you like most? Why?

_____

_____

_____

_____

_____

_____

_____

_____

_____

_____

How did your views on money change as you got older?

When it comes to education and working, what is your most valuable advice for me?

a page for
pictures . . .

. . . and more stories
and memories

a page for
pictures . . .

. . . and more stories
and memories

TELL ME SOMETHING
ABOUT ME

What was I like as a child?

Who did
I resemble
more, you
or Mum?

Did you have a pet name for me?

What did you like most about me as a child?

Which memories from when I was young bring a smile to your face?

TELL ME SOMETHING
ABOUT ME

How do I remind you of your parents?

Did I resemble you more or less as I grew up?

How can
you tell?

What was my favourite food? What food did I hate?

What did I like most about my birthdays?

Do you remember what I thought of my first day of school?

TELL ME SOMETHING
ABOUT ME

What family trips or holidays were special to me? _____

_____

_____

_____

_____

_____

_____

_____

_____

_____

_____

_____

_____

What music did I like when I was little? _____

_____

_____

_____

_____

_____

_____

_____

_____

What did I want to be when I was grown up?

What was I like as a teenager? What was the hardest part about that time for you?

And what was
the best part?

a page for
pictures . . .

... and more stories
and memories

GROWING
UP

ABOUT LOVE

Who was your first crush? When and where did you meet? _____

_____

_____

_____

_____

_____

_____

Who was your first kiss? Did you enjoy the experience? _____

_____

_____

_____

_____

_____

_____

Did you find it easy to talk to your crushes, or were you very shy? _____

_____

_____

_____

_____

_____

_____

Who gave you 'the talk'? How old were you?

Who was your first true love?

How did
you two
meet?

ABOUT LOVE

Have you had many love interests? _____

_____

_____

_____

_____

_____

_____

Did you ever suffer a broken heart? _____

_____

_____

How did you
cope with it? _____

_____

_____

_____

_____

_____

_____

_____

_____

What was the most original or fun way somebody let you know

you were special to them?

How and when did you meet my mother?

Was there
an instant
attraction?

69

ABOUT LOVE

Where did you go on your first date? _____

_____

Were you very
nervous?

_____

_____

_____

_____

When did you really start to fall for her? _____

_____

_____

_____

_____

_____

_____

_____

What did you like most about her?

What did your parents think of her?

Did they
approve of
your choice?

ABOUT LOVE

Did you propose? How? _____

_____

_____

_____

_____

_____

_____

_____

_____

What was your wedding day like? _____

_____

_____

_____

_____

_____

_____

_____

How long have you two been together? _____

_____

_____

_____

What is your best advice for maintaining a healthy relationship?

And what are the biggest pitfalls in a relationship?

a page for
pictures . . .

. . . and more stories
and memories

a page for
pictures . . .

. . . and more stories
and memories

ABOUT BECOMING
A FATHER

Have you always wanted to be a dad?

Was there a
moment you
knew you
were ready
for it?

How did you find out you were going to be a dad?

Do you remember how it made you feel?

How did you feel about the pregnancy?

Did you go to
any classes
with Mum, for
example?

What was important to you both when it came to raising me?

ABOUT BECOMING
A FATHER

Did you know whether I was going to be a boy or a girl? _____

_____

_____

_____

_____

_____

_____

_____

_____

_____

Was it an easy pregnancy? _____

_____

What did you
want to do
differently from
your parents?
And what did you
want to do exactly
the same?

_____

_____

_____

_____

_____

Did your relationship with your parents change when you became a father?

How do you remember the day I was born?

Did you
celebrate?

ABOUT BECOMING
A FATHER

Which people were important to you after my birth?

_____

_____

_____

_____

_____

_____

_____

_____

How did your life change after you had me?

_____

_____

_____

_____

_____

_____

_____

_____

How did fatherhood change you?

What did you like most about being a father? And least?

a page for
pictures . . .

. . . and more stories
and memories

a page for
pictures . . .

. . . and more stories
and memories

TELL ME SOMETHING
ABOUT ME

Do you remember who my first love was? What did you think of him/her? _____

_____

_____

_____

_____

_____

_____

_____

_____

Did I behave differently when I was in love? _____

Did that change with each new crush? _____

_____

_____

_____

_____

_____

_____

_____

_____

What is your best advice when it comes to raising children?

Raising me, is there anything you would do differently now,

if you had the chance?

TELL ME SOMETHING
ABOUT ME

Considering everything I've learned from you, _____

what are you most proud of having taught me?_____

_____

_____

_____

_____

_____

_____

_____

_____

_____

_____

_____

_____

_____

_____

_____

_____

_____

_____

What has the experience of raising me taught you?

a page for
pictures . . .

. . . and more stories
and memories

ALL
YOUR
FAVOURITES

ABOUT SPARE TIME,
HOBBIES AND TRAVELLING

How do you like to spend your weekends?

How did you like to spend your weekends when you were younger?

How old were
you when
you started
going out?

What were your favourite hangouts?

Who did
you go
out with?

What are some of your favourite memories from back then?

ABOUT SPARE TIME,
HOBBIES AND TRAVELLING

How do you spend your free time?

Do you enjoy reading?

What
are your
favourite
books?

What was the first film you saw in the cinema?

What are your favourite films?

What makes you so excited you'd drop everything to talk about it?

ABOUT SPARE TIME,
HOBBIES AND TRAVELLING

What are your favourite television programmes? _____

_____

_____

_____

And which
ones make you
reach for the
remote?

_____

_____

_____

_____

_____

_____

_____

If you could eat at any restaurant, which one would you choose? _____

_____

_____

_____

_____

_____

_____

_____

_____

_____

_____

_____

What is your favourite food?

What are your favourite travel destinations?

ABOUT SPARE TIME, HOBBIES AND TRAVELLING

When you're on holiday, what do you miss from home?

_____

What was one of your best trips? Why?

_____

And which holiday was just plain awful? What happened?

Which places do you feel everyone should visit at least once in their lifetime?

ABOUT SPARE TIME, HOBBIES AND TRAVELLING

What music never fails to cheer you up? _____

_____

_____

_____

_____

_____

_____

_____

_____

_____

_____

What is the best or most beautiful thing about the country where you live? _____

_____

_____

_____

_____

_____

_____

_____

_____

_____

_____

_____

What would you do if you won a million pounds?

a page for
pictures . . .

. . . and more stories
and memories

a page for
pictures . . .

. . . and more stories
and memories

TELL ME SOMETHING ABOUT ME

What was our first holiday together like? Where did we go? _____

_____
_____
_____
_____
_____
_____
_____
_____
_____
_____

What things would you still like to see or do with me? _____

_____
_____

Why these
things in
particular?

_____
_____
_____
_____
_____

_____ Did you read to me when I was young?

_____ Which books were my favourites?

_____

_____

_____

_____

_____

_____

_____

_____

_____

_____

_____ Is there anything you think I should absolutely read,

_____ listen to or do when I get the chance?

_____

_____

_____

_____

_____

_____

_____

a page for
pictures . . .

. . . and more stories
and memories

a page for
pictures . . .

. . . and more stories
and memories

WHO
YOU ARE
NOW

ABOUT MEMORIES

Is there a particular song, scent or something else that never _____

fails to remind you of something wonderful? _____

_____

_____

_____

_____

_____

_____

_____

_____

_____

Which of your dreams came true? _____

_____

Which of
your dreams
would you still
like to
come true? _____

_____

_____

_____

Which of your accomplishments in life makes you feel proud?

What would you still like to accomplish?

What life lesson would you like to pass on to me?

ABOUT MEMORIES

Is there a joke or funny memory that still makes you laugh to this day? _____

_____

_____

_____

_____

_____

_____

_____

What are the best decisions you've made in your life? _____

_____

_____

_____

_____

_____

_____

_____

_____

_____

_____

What obstacles have you overcome in your life?

How did
you do this?

ABOUT MEMORIES

What are your regrets, big or small? _____

_____

_____

_____

_____

_____

_____

_____

_____

What is the best resolution you ever made? _____

_____

_____

_____

_____

_____

_____

_____

If you had the chance, which moments in your life

would you like to live all over again?

What do you think are the most remarkable events in history

that happened during your life?

ABOUT MEMORIES

Which historical figures do you admire?

_____

Which people in your life do you owe a lot to?

Who did you
learn the
most from?

What is the biggest difference between who you used to be and

who you are now?

Were there any important people in your life you had to say goodbye to?

How did
you deal
with that
loss?

a page for
pictures . . .

a page for
pictures . . .

. . . and more stories
and memories

ABOUT THOUGHTS,
WISHES AND DREAMS

What do you think are the most important things in life?

How important is your home to you?

What's your
favourite spot
at home?

Who serves as an inspiration to you?

Why this
person?

Which famous people do you admire?

ABOUT THOUGHTS, WISHES AND DREAMS

Which days of the year are important to you? _____

_____

_____

_____

How do you
like to spend
these days? _____

_____

_____

_____

_____

_____

_____

_____

And which traditions do you love? _____

_____

_____

_____

_____

_____

_____

_____

_____

_____

What does happiness mean to you?

Did you
always look
at it that
way?

What are your best qualities?

ABOUT THOUGHTS,
WISHES AND DREAMS

What would you change about yourself if you could?

What things would you still like to learn?

What do you think are some of the benefits of growing older?

What makes you howl with laughter?

ABOUT THOUGHTS,
WISHES AND DREAMS

What things really move you? _____

_____

_____

_____

_____

_____

_____

_____

_____

What is your favourite day of the week? And your favourite month of the year? _____

_____

_____

_____

_____

_____

_____

_____

If you could rule the world for one day, what would be your first decision?

In what ways has the world changed as you have grown older?

ABOUT THOUGHTS, WISHES AND DREAMS

What does friendship mean to you? _____

_____

_____

_____

Who are your
best friends?
Why is that? _____

_____

_____

_____

_____

_____

_____

_____

What is the greatest gift someone could give you? _____

_____

_____

_____

_____

_____

_____

_____

_____

_____

Who helps you pull through when life gets tough?

What is one of the biggest compliments you have ever received?

ABOUT THOUGHTS, WISHES AND DREAMS

What places or countries would you still like to visit? _____

_____

_____

_____

_____

_____

_____

_____

Looking back, what were the greatest moments in your life? _____

_____

_____

_____

_____

_____

_____

_____

_____

_____

_____

_____

_____

Which great moments are still to come?

Is there anything you would still like to tell me?

a page for
pictures . . .

. . . and more stories
and memories

a page for
pictures . . .

... and more stories
and memories

TELL ME SOMETHING
ABOUT ME

Which of my choices makes you proud? _____

What have you learned from me?

Which of our moments together would you pick

if you could go back and relive them?

TELL ME SOMETHING ABOUT ME

What is the most wonderful thing about our relationship? _____

What would make it even better? _____

_____

_____

_____

_____

_____

Are there any questions you would like to ask me? _____

_____

_____

_____

_____

_____

_____

_____

_____

_____

_____

_____

_____ What dreams do you have for me?

a page for
pictures . . .

. . . and more stories
and memories

PARTICULAR BOOKS

UK | USA | Canada | Ireland | Australia
India | New Zealand | South Africa

Penguin Books is part of the Penguin Random House group of companies
whose addresses can be found at global.penguinrandomhouse.com.

First published in the Netherlands as *Pap, vertel eens* by Spectrum,
an imprint of Uitgeverij Unieboek, Houten 2015
First published in Great Britain by Particular Books 2020
001

Printed and bound in Italy by LEGO S.p.A.

A CIP catalogue record for this book is available from the British Library

ISBN: 978–0–241–44929–5

www.greenpenguin.co.uk

MIX
Paper from
responsible sources
FSC
www.fsc.org   FSC® C018179

Penguin Random House is committed to a
sustainable future for our business, our readers
and our planet. This book is made from Forest
Stewardship Council® certified paper.